Anxiety and _____

In the shadow's of a restless mind,
Anxiety weaves a web, unkind.
Whispers of doubt, a constant stream,
A haunting presence, a recurring dream.

Depression's weight, a heavy cloak,
Dulling colours, like silent smoke.
A dance with shadow's, a restless face,
In the heart's darkness, emotions ebb and flow.

Yet, within the storm, a glimmer may be found,
A resilient spirit, though silently bound.
Seeking solace, in the quiet night,
A fragile hope, a flickering light.

The struggle painted in shades of grey,
Yet courage lingers, day by day.
In the depths, a resilience so deep,
A gradual climb, a journey to reap.

So, hold on tight, through the darkest night,
For in the morning, there may be light.
Anxiety and depression, a turbulent sea,
But within, a strength, yearning to be free.

Hunter of the Night

In shadow's soft, where moonlight weaves,
A feline prowls, among the leaves.
Whisker's twitch, eyes gleam bright,
Silent hunter of the night.

A coat of velvet, sleep and black,
Paws that dance along the track.
Graceful leaps, a silent chase,
In moonlit night, a silent embrace.

Eyes that sparkle with mystery,
Reflecting stars in symphony.
A gentle purr, a soothing sound,
In moonlit silence, joy is found.

Whispers of a feline grace,
Echo softly in the quiet space.
A mystic dance, a whiskered sprite,
A moonlit cat, a charming sight.

Memories
For Alex.

In the quiet chambers of his mind,
A gentle dance, memories entwined.
A father once, strong and wise,
Now lost beneath forgetful skies.

Alzheimer's, a restless tide,
Stealing moments, a silent guide.
Yet in the shadows, a love persists,
A bond unspoken, though memories twist.

Through the labyrinth of fading thought,
A son's love, tirelessly sought.
In every smile, a fleeting trace,
Of the man he was, in a distant space.

Whispers of stories, like autumn leaves,
Cradled in the heart, where love believes.
A son's hand, a steadfast guide,
Navigating shores, where memories hide.

In the twilight of the challenging quest,
A father's essence, still manifest.
Though the word's may falter, the eyes may dim,
Love's language transcends, reaching within.

So, in the dance of each passing day,
A son cherishes moments, come what may.
For in the heart's treasury, memories align,
A son's love, a forever lifeline.

Chaos, but Fun.

In the chaos of toys, and bedtime strife,
Raising kids is a wild, comical life.
Nappies, tantrums and sticky faces,
Parenting antics in all the right places.

Tiny tornadoes, a whirlwind of cheer,
Every day brings something to laugh at or jeer.
Mismatched socks and spaghetti on walls,
Parenting's a ride, the greatest of all.

Naptime battles, a war of the wills,
Trying to count all those bedtime thrills.
Juice spills and giggles, laughter so loud,
Parenting's a circus, make no mistake, be proud.

From ABC's, to tying a shoe,
Every milestone a victory, it's true.
Wrestling with laundry, a never-ending bout,
Parenting humour, that's what it's about.

Teaching them to share and play nice,
Like a stand-up comic, repeating advice.
Endless questions, why? Without end,
Parenting's a script, with loops and bends.

But in the midst of chaos and bedtime tales,
Come hugs and kisses, the sweetest of trails.
A funny journey, a joyous endeavour,
Raising kids, its laughter forever.

Love and Romance

In the tapestry of life, a twist unfolds,
A story of love, in hues untold.
Unexpectedly, like a soft sunrise,
Romance blossoms, a sweet surprise.

Fate weaves threads in a subtle dance,
Two hearts entwined, a serendipitous chance.
Eyes meet, and in that fleeting moment,
Love awakens, in a sweet, silent blaze.

A chance encounter, a fateful embrace,
In the heart's garden, a tender space.
Whispers of love, in the gentle breeze,
A symphony of moments, crafted to please.

Unseen forces guides hearts' tender flight,
Kindred spirits drawn together in the night.
Love found in places unforeseen,
A magical dance, a destiny keen.

So, cherish the moments, love's sweet decree,
For in unexpected places, love may be.
A tale of romance, beautifully spun,
In the dance of hearts, two become one.

The Empty Chair.

Beneath the twinkling Christmas lights so bright,
A void echoes in the silent night.
A chair left empty, a presence gone,
A missing loved one, in the holiday dawn.

Snowflakes dance in a melancholy ballet,
As memories of laughter softly sway.
The warmth of love, a cherished glow,
Yet, shadows linger in the falling snow.

Familiar carols ring through the air,
But a bittersweet melody, a subtle despair.
The scent of pine and cinnamon cheer,
Yet, a lingering absence whispers near.

In the glow of candles, a solemn prayer,
For the one who's absent, a love to hear.
A toast to joy, a nod to pain,
In the heart's silence, love remains.

Gifts wrapped with care, yet one undone,
A token for the absent, the cherished one.
Through miles apart, in spirit they stay,
A missing presence, on this Christmas day.

Through tearful smiles and a tender embrace,
Love transcends time, a comforting grace.
In the tapestry of memories spun,
A missing loved one, forever a cherished one.

Heroes'

In Shield's embrace, a hero stands,
Captain America, shield in hand.
Bucky Barnes, a loyal friend,
Through battles fought, they won't bend.

In frozen echoes of the past,
A friendship forged, forever to last.
Bucky's arm, a metal grace,
A bond unbroken, that can't erase.

Through wartime strife and modern days,
In star-spangled glory, friendship stays.
Two soldiers strong, side by side,
In freedom's name, they'll always bide.

Winter

Whispers of frost in the quiet morn,
Icy tendrils on branches born.
Nestled in blankets, the world in sleep,
The hush of snowfall, secrets to keep,
Each flake a dancer in the crisp, cold air.
Rooflines adorned with a silvery glare.

Autumn

Amber leaves in a gentle descent,
Under the boughs, a rustic tent.
The air with a chill, a whispering name,
Unveiling colours through the trees.
Mellow golds and reds, a painters delight,
Nature's canvas in the fading light.

Spring

Soft petals bloom in the morning light,
Perfumed air, a sweet delight.
Robins sing in a symphony,
Inspiring life in every tree.
Nestled bds unfurls with grace,
Gentle showers, natures embrace.

Summer

Sunshine paints the sky in hues,
Underneath it's warm embrace, we cruise.
Mirthful laugher, children's play,
Meadows bloom in the light of day.
Evenings draped in a golden gleam,
Revelling in summer's blissful dream.

A Loved One

In dawn's first light, a melody begins,
Robin's arrive, their joyous hymns.
Feathers brushed with the morning sun,
A reunion with a loved one has begun.

Whispers of tales from lands afar,
Carried on wings like a shooting star.
Their song, a greeting in the quiet morn,
A visitor cherished, a connection reborn.

In the garden, a dance with delight,
As memories flutter in the warm daylight.
A symphony shared, a bond profound,
With each sweet note, love echoes around.

Two Sisters.
For my little sister.

In laughter shared and secrets sealed,
Two sister's bond, a love revealed.
Through childhood dreams and teenage years,
A symphony of joy, a chorus of tears.

Side by side, they face life's climb,
A dance of season's, sweet and prime.
Sister's whispers in the night,
Guiding stars, their shared light.

In differences found strength unfold,
Yet hearts entwined in a love so bold.
With open arms and understanding gaze,
Through life's maze, in sisterhood, embrace.

Hand in hand, they navigate,
The twists of fate, the turns of fate.
Through every trial, each sunny day,
Sisters stand, come what may.

Mischievous Magpie's

In the city's hustle, where buildings scrape the sky,
Magpies strut the sidewalks, oh my, oh my.
With feathers glossy, black and white,
They're comedians of avian sight.

Scheming magpies in feathered caper,
Collecting shiny bits, a gleaming paper.
Hitching rides on the trash-can express,
Wings a flutter in a feathery mess.

In the morning's quiet, they hold a conference,
Chirps and cackles, a raucous insistence.
Discussing secrets in a huddle so sly,
Magpies, the gossipers of the urban sky.

But when they sun sets, and the day is done,
They gather, a parliament, under the sun.
In the moonlit party of the midnight trees,
Magpies chuckle with the greatest of ease.

A Butterfly's Tale

In the field's of sorrow, where shadows weep,
Butterflies dance, a memory to keep.
Silken wings, fragile and light,
Fluttering whispers in the tear-stained night.

Cocooned dreams, once vibrant and fair,
Now aching echoes in the evening air.
Transformation of joy to pain,
Butterfly's weep in the summer rain.

Each fluttering wing, a sigh released,
A gentle touch where heartache increased.
Colours fading, like the setting sun,
Butterfly's mourn what can't be undone.

Amidst the blooms, a poignant ballet,
Silent tears in the soft decay.
In the garden of loss, where emotions fly,
Butterflies weep, beneath the weeping sky.

I am Not Gone

In the quiet space where shadows linger,
A spirit hovers, a gentle wisp of a finger.
Gazing upon the loved ones left behind,
A spectre of solace, in heartache, they find.

Through tears that fall like gentle rain,
The departed watches, their love sustained.
In the candle's glow, and the flickering flame,
Whispers echo, though none speak the name.

"I am not gone; I'm in the starry night,
A celestial dance, a shimmering light.
Feel me in the breeze that softly sighs,
In every dawn, where the sun will rise".

The mourning hearts, heavy with sorrow,
Feel a presence, a promise for tomorrow.
In memories cherished, in laughter and pain,
The departed lingers, forever to remain.

"I am the whisper in the rustling leaves,
A gentle reminder that never truly leaves.
In your dreams, I'll softly tread,
A tender presence beside your bed."

With love unseen, a comforting embrace,
The departed consoles, leaving a trace.
In the tapestry of grief, threads of hope,
A celestial connection, an eternal rope.

An 80's Childhood

In the late 80's, a child's world began,
A time of innocence, a simpler plan.
Neon bright, and big hairdo's,
The tape deck rhythm, the radio's prose.

Cabbage patch kids and Teddy Ruxpin tales,
Jelly shoes clicking on pavement trails.
Break dancing moves on cardboard floors,
A childhood of memories, all to adore.

Rubik's Cube twisting in curious hands,
Hula Hoops twirling a backyard sands.
Funky fresh fashion, colours so bold,
A treasure trove of memories to behold.

Pac-man patterns in the arcade glow,
Nintendo challenges, an endless flow.
A Walkman playing the latest hit,
In the 80's echo, a child's spirit in it.

Schoolyard games and friendship bands,
Skateboard's rolling in suburban lands.
Carefree days, oh, how they flew,
A late 80's childhood, forever true.

To A 90's Teen

In the early 90's, a girl began to play,
In a world of neon, where innocence had sway.
With scrunchies high, and denim wide,
Her childhood unfurled like a colourful tide.

Tales spun on a cassette, rewind and play,
Hopscotch on pavements, a bright sunny day.
Pigtails and barrettes, a fashion parade,
In the 90's dance, memories were made.

Saturday cartoons, on the living room screen,
Dial up tones and MSN dreams.
Rollerblades humming out on the street,
A mixture of laughter, a rhythm so sweet.

Walkman melodies, in a pocket snug,
In the backyard, catching some lady bugs.
Lunchables stacked in a rainbow array,
A taste of nostalgia in the light of day.

Gameboy adventures and Tetris highs,
In the glow of street lights, beneath midnight skies.
A world of wonder, simple and free,
A 90's childhood in reverie.

Halloween Party

In the moonlit night of pumpkin delight,
Halloween giggles take flight.
Witches cackling, brooms in a spin,
A comedy of costume, let the fun begin!

Ghosts practice their "boo" in the dark,
Skeletons attempt a dance with a spark.
Zombie's grooving to a spooky dance,
In the laughter-filled graveyard, they chance.

Vampires trying to look scary and chic,
But fumbling with their capes, oh, how unique.
Werewolves practicing their howls in time,
Tripping over paws under the haunted moon.

Candy wrappers rustle in the eerie breeze,
Mummies unwrapping, trying to appease.
Jack O' Lanterns grinning, toothy and bright,
Sharing jokes that go bump in the night.

A laughter potion in the witches brew,
Giggles contagious, spreading like flu.
Halloween mirth, a bewitching spell,
A graveyard party, all is well!

Christmas Morning

In the hushed tones of the night,
The child dreams awake.
Visions of tinsel and twinkling lights,
In their small heart, anticipation takes.

Through the window, a silent snowfall,
A blanket for the world to borrow.
The moon, a pale witness to the child's delight,
As they wait for the morrow.

Imagination a flutter, like paper snowflakes,
The room adorned, with a special glow.
Stockings hanging, patiently awaiting,
A secret dance, only they know.

In the quiet hum of Christmas Eve,
The child's pulse matches the fireplace's ember.
Gifts wrapped in dreams, waiting to unfold,
In the enchanting alchemy of December.

Sleep tiptoes on the edge of eyelids,
While the child counts reindeer in the sky.
Christmas mornings, a whispered promise,
Of wonders unfurling, as the dawn draws nigh.

Growing Old

Through the passages of fleeting time,
A couple weathers life's rhythmic chime.
Hand in hand, as the years unfold,
In the tapestry of love, their story told.

Youthful laughter echoes in shared gaze,
Lines etched with memories, a life ablaze.
Silver strands among the familiar gold,
A journey written, as the years are scrolled.

Weathered hands, fingers interlaced,
Each crease a chapter, an enduring embrace.
Eyes that spark, with tales untold,
In the symphony of aging, their love takes hold.

Through seasons danced, in joy and strife,
They've navigated the tapestry of life.
Together, they've weathered the sun and storm,
In the gentle grace of growing old, a uniform.

With every twinkle, a laughter line,
A testament to the love, divine.
In the twilight's glow, where dreams unfold,
A couple grows old, their love ever bold.

A woman's Journey.

In the threads of time, a woman's journey unfolds,
From childhood's laughter to stories yet untold.
A girl, wide-eyed, with dreams unfurled,
Chasing butterflies in a whimsical world.

Teenage years, a symphony of highs and lows,
A dance with passion, a path she chosen.
In the mirrors reflection, adolescence weaves,
A kaleidoscope of hopes and believes.

Into womanhood, she steps with grace,
Naughty life's tumultuous embrace.
In the tapestry of choices, joy and strife,
She paints her canvas with colours of life.

Through seasons of love, with heartbeats wild,
A woman blossoms, as lover and child.
In the crucible time, maturity's embrace,
She finds her rhythm, her unique grace.

Menopause, a transition, a shift in the tide,
Yet, she faces it with courage and pride.
A metamorphosis, an ageless flame,
A woman, resilient, never the same.

With silver strands, a crown of years,
She embraces wisdom, conquers fear.
In the autumn of life, where memories bloom,
She savours the richness, dispelling the gloom.

In the final act, as the curtain gently falls,
She wears her wrinkles like heirlooms on the walls.
A life well-lived, a story to be told,
A woman, aging gracefully, growing old.

Bonnie Scotland

Beneath the sky of heathered hue,
When ancient echoes linger true.
Scotland's beauty, a timeless grace,
A land where dreams and legends embrace.

Rolling hills of emerald green,
A portrait painted, so serene.
Majestic castles, tales untold,
Whispers in the misty world.

Lochs that mirror the tranquil sky,
Reflect the soul, where eagles fly.
Bagpipes playing, a haunting tune,
Beneath the waning, Highland moon.

Heather blooms, in shades of heath,
A tapestry woven, a land beneath.
Friendly faces, warm and kind,
In Scotland's hearts, a rare design.

Edinburgh's skyline, a historic crown,
With cobblestone streets worn smooth,
renowned.
Glasgow's spirit, vibrant and bold,
A tale of resilience, proudly told.

From the Isles to the Grampian Park,
Scotland's magic, a language unique.
In every glen, on each bonnie brae,
A piece of heaven, forever to stay.

Anne Boleyn

In Tudor's halls, where whispers weave,
A tale of Anne, the crowned to grieve.
A tempestuous era, a throne to sway,
Anne Boleyn, in the court's ballet.

Her gaze, a spark in Henry's eye,
Ambition soared, ambition to vie.
A queen in waiting, ambitions and shrewd,
In the chessboard of power, her moves pursued.

With dark-eyed charm, a captivating spell,
Anne's rise in court, a story to tell.
A tempestuous courtship, clandestine and wild,
Yet, destiny's dance is a fickle child.

Marriage vows spoken, coronations glean,
A queen's ascent, a turbulent dream.
The Tudor's shadow, a sombre decree,
Anne Boleyn, a tragic legacy.

Whispers of treason, in the courtly air,
Innocence tarnished, beyond repair.
Her scaffold awaits, the axe's decree,
A queen condemned, in history decree.

Yet, Anne's legacy lingers in history embrace,
A queen whose spirit refuses to efface.
In the pages of time, her story told,
Anne Boleyn, a queen, both fierce and bold.

The Six Wives of Henry VIII

Catherine of Aragon, a Spanish rose,
Wed to Henry, their love story chose.
Yet, barren whispers, an heir elusive cry,
Their union faltered, a bitter goodbye.

Anne Boleyn, with eyes that could enthral,
A queen who rose, then faced the fall.
Charged with treason, on the scaffold's stage,
She left the throne, a history's page.

Jane Seymour, in quiet grace,
Gave Henry a son, an heir to trace.
Yet, her life, too, met a fleeting fate,
In shadows cast, by a royal mate.

Anne of Cleves, a foreign bride,
Marriage ended as quickly as the "I do".
Divorced, not beheaded, she stepped aside,
In the grand spectacle, a royal divide.

Catherine Howard, youth's allure,
Yet secrets hidden, love impure.
Accused of dalliance, a tragic drama,
Her youth extinguished, beneath Tudor skies.

Catherine Parr, the final queen,
Widowed twice, her fate serene.
An author and stepmother in royal grace,
She closed the chapter in history's embrace.

Six wives entwined in Henry's fate,

A saga told by the hands of fate.
In England's annals, their stories unfold,
The six wives of Henry, a tale to be told.

The Avengers

In the realm where heroes unite,
A saga unfolds, in cosmic light.
Avenger's assemble, a valiant crew,
A symphony of power, a justice true.

Ironclad genius, in red and gold,
Tony Stark's take, in brilliance told.
A heart of arc reactor, a genius mind,
In the armours embrace, courage defined.

Thor, the God of Thunder's might,
Mjolnir's dance in the Asgardian night.
A cosmic warrior with a regal stand,
Guardians of realms, across the land.

Captain America, a symbol of grace,
A shield's defence, an unyielding embrace.
In red, white and blue, freedom's call,
A soldier's spirit, standing tall.

Natasha Romanoff, a shadow's dance,
In the spy's intrigue, a deadly romance.
Widow's bite and past concealed,
A hero's heart, never revealed.

Hulk, the behemoth with a gentle soul,
A scientists rage, a gamma-fuelled toll.
Green giants strength, in battle roars,
In Bruce Banner's struggle, redemption soars.

Hawkeye, the archer with arrows keen,

A marksman aim, in battles unseen.
In purple colours, a steadfast bow,
A hero's path, in every arrows glow.

Together, they stand, a force untamed,
Against threats that leave the world inflamed.
In the Avengers anthem, courage thrives,
A team of heroes', where hope survives.

The Scottish Weather.

In Scotland's land, where thistles sway,
The weather tells a tale each day.
The sky, a patchwork o' silver and grey,
Speaks Scots, in wind's wild, wuthering play.

O'er heathered hills and glens sae green,
The winds a braw and blusterin' queen.
She dances through the glens and braes,
Unfurling secrets in her airy maze.

The rain, a fine and misty cloak,
Gars moors and lochs in driechness soak.
Yet, in this dear, a beauty lies,
As droplets dance, 'neath weepin' skies.

On mountains high, a snowy braw,
A winter's touch, a white-clad law.
The clouds like tartan, weave and wend,
In Scotland's skies, an ever-changin' blend.

So, in Scots, the weather's tale unfolds,
In moody skies, where mystery holds.
In every gust and raindrops glee,
Scotland's weather sings in Scots, wild and free.

Edinburgh

In Edinburgh's heart, where tales are spun,
A city old, 'neath a castle's watchful sun.
Cobbled streets and whispers in the breeze,
Edinburgh's charm, a timeless tease.

From Arthur's seat, the view unfold,
A skyline etched in stories, untold.
Café's hum with laughter, warm and bright,
In every wynd, a secret takes flight.

The Royal Mile, a historic stride,
With echoes of the past, side by side.
Greyfriars's Bobby, a loyal friend,
In Edinburgh's tale, a steadfast blend.

Beneath the tattoo of the piper's song,
Edinburgh's spirits marches strong.
A city proud, where dreams ignite,
In twilights glow, a magic light.

Queen Elizabeth II, A tribute.

In regal grace, Queen Elizabeth stands,
A monarch's reign over distant lands.
Crowned in duty, with a steadfast mien,
Her presence echoes serene and keen.

Through era's shifting, with wisdom's gaze,
She guided a kingdom through historic days.
A sovereign's heart, a nations pride,
In royal robes, she did preside.

With dignity, she wore the crown,
In palace walls, and far-renowned.
A symbol of continuity,
Queen Elizabeth, Her Royal Majesty.

A Mother's Love

In the quiet hush of twilight's embrace,
A mother's love, a boundless grace.
Tender whispers, like a lullaby's song,
In her embrace, where hearts belong.

Through sleepless nights and daylight's glow,
Her love, a river that continues to flow.
In every tear, in every sweet embrace,
A mother's love, a sacred space.

Through joys and sorrow, thick and thin,
Her love, a constant, like a dawn's soft grin.
Unseen, yet felt in each heartbeat's hum,
A mother's love, forever and some.

In laughter shared and dreams unfurled,
A mother's love, the dearest in the world.
A gentle force that will not part,
Eternal love, a masterpiece of the heart.

Siblings

In the garden of kin, where bonds are sown,
Siblings love, a melody al their own.
Through laughter shared and secrets kept,
A lifelong friendship, in each step.

Brothers and sisters, side by side,
In the dance of time, their spirits guide.
A patchwork quilt of memories weave,
In the heart, where kinship conceives.

Through storms and sunshine, hand in hand,
Siblings traverse the shifting sand.
A constellation of shared history,
Bound by love, an unspoken mystery.

Musical Emotions

In notes that dance, a melody untold,
Music whispers stories, both young and old.
A symphony of emotions, a vibrant hue,
It paints the canvas of the soul, anew.

With every chord, memories awake,
A nostalgia journey, a timeless lake.
Through rhythmic waves, emotions rise,
In the melody's embrace, the heart complies.

Lifting on wings of a harmonious flight,
Music elevates, a celestial light.
It weaves through time, a timeless thread,
Guiding the heart where memories are bred.

In the crescendo, tears may flow,
A cascade of emotions, an ebb and flow.
Yet, in the sob of a well-played song,
A healing balm, where the heart belongs.

Strumming the strings of joy and sorrow,
Music echoes a promise of a better tomorrow.
It's a language that needs no words,
A symphony of feelings, a songbirds choice.

So, let the music play, let it soar,
In its embrace, our spirits implore.
For in each note, a story lies,
A serenade that made the soul arise.

Freedom of Flight.

Through the azure expanse, I take flight,
Wings of dreams catching the sun's soft light.
Upward, I soar on a whimsical light,
Amongst the clouds, where dreams touch the sky.

The endless blue unfolds below,
A world left behind, in a graceful flow.
Whispers of wind, a gentle caress,
As I navigate through the vastness.

Feathers of courage, my wings now wear,
I leave behind doubts, suspended in air.
Closer to heaven, where freedom is heard,
I become one with the winged, a liberated bird.

Through the heaven's my spirit takes flight,
A dance with the stars, in the soft twilight.
Gravity's grasp no longer confined,
In the open sky, true freedom, I find.

Lost in A Book

In the quiet land of painted dreams,
A world unfurls, or so it seems.
Pages turn, a gentle embrace,
As reality fades, I find my space.

Characters breathe, emotions bloom,
In the cocoon of a well-woven loom.
Lust in words, I wonder far,
Beyond the reach of the world's memoir.

Each sentence a pathway, a secret door,
Into world's untold, forevermore.
Imagination takes its glorious flight,
In the magic of words, I find my light.

Time elopes, as chapters unfold,
A story whispered, a treasure to hold.
In the tapestry of tale, I am spun,
A journey begun, never to be undone.

Through the valley's of prose, I roam,
In the cathedrals of language, I find home.
Lost, not in chaos, but in sweet surrender,
A books embrace, gentle and tender.

A symphony of sentences, an epic ballet,
In the boundless expanse, I drift away.
For in the dance of words, a truth is shook,
The enchantment lies in getting lost, in a book.

Colours of the Rainbow.

In the canvas of the sky, a rainbow gleams,
A prism of feelings in seven radiant streams.
Red pulses with passion, a fiery desire,
A spark in the heart, an emotional fire.

Orange beams warmth, like a comforting
embrace,
A glow of joy, a sunlit space.
Yellow exudes cheer, a vibrant sunbeam,
A burst of happiness, like a golden dream.

Green breathes calm, in natures soft embrace,
A tranquil melody, a soothing grace.
Blue echoes serenity, the tranquil sea,
A gentle whisper, where the soul feels free.

Indigo holds depth, like a twilight hue,
A quiet mystery, a subtle cue.
Violet dreams in the twilights glow,
A poetic sigh, where fantasies flow.

Each colour a note in emotions song,
In the arc of the rainbow, feelings belong.
Together they weave, a spectrum so wide,
In hues of the heart, emotions reside.

The Sock Mystery.

In the laundry room of life, a mystery unfolds,
A tale of socks, vanishing, in laundry's holds.
Pairs once united, now torn asunder,
The sock saga begins, a mystery, a wonder.

Into the washing machine, they gleefully dive,
In a soapy adventure, where socks connive.
Spin cycle antics, a while escapade,
Socks play hide and seek in the laundry arcade.

One sock emerges with a mischievous grin,
It's partner lost, inside the linen bin.
The solo act in the sock drawer parade,
The other sock left behind, feeling betrayed.

In the tumble dryer's warm embrace,
Socks pirouette in a waltz of grace.
But one decides to play a prank,
Leaving it's twin in the laundry tank.

Behind the sofa, beneath the bed,
Sock hideouts where they've secretly fled.
A sock safari, a guest to reclaim,
Missing pairs, in a new laundry game.

Mismatched socks become the trend,
A fashion statement, a sock blend.
Striped with polka dots, a crazy array,
Laundry's mischievous ballet.

So, next time you ponder the sock conundrum,

Remember, you're in the laundry's kingdom.
Socks embark on a solo mission,
A whimsical tale, of sock superstition.

The Tale of Friendship

In the garden of life, where moments bloom,
Friendships a flower, banishing gloom.
A shared laughter, a comforting smile,
In the book of companionship, page by joyous mail.

Through sunlit days and moonlit nights,
Friendship weaves it's magic, soaring heights.
A bond unspoken, a silent embrace,
A sanctuary of trust, a comforting space.

In storms of sorrow or joyous weather,
Friends stand strong, tethered together.
A symphony of hearts, a harmonious blend,
Through twists and turns, a friendship to men.

In the dance of time, hand in hand,
Friends create memories, a treasure grand.
A constellation of moments, shining bright,
Friendship, a beacon in the darkest night.

A Sunrise

In the quiet embrace of dawn's soft light,
Sunrise paints the sky in colours so bright.
Love, a sunrise in the heart's expanse,
A radiant glow, a timeless dance.

As the sun emerges, a golden kiss,
Love awakens, a moment of bliss.
In the beauty of morning, colours above,
Sunrise and love, a symphony of endless love.

A Sunset

In the horizon's farewell, the sun descends,
A palette of hues, where daylight ends.
In the twilights embrace, shadow's grow,
A cosmic goodbye, a celestial show.

Like the sun, life bows to the night,
In the sunset of existence, a poignant sight.
Yet, in the dusk, a promise is spun,
For the night, new stories have begun,

Intimacy

In the quiet spaces where whispers reside,
Intimacy blossoms, a tender tide.
A language beyond words, a silent song,
In the sacred dance where two hearts belong.

Skin to skin, an intimate ballet,
Fingers tracing secrets, a private display.
Eyes locking in a gaze profound,
In the intimacy's haven, emotions unbound.

Vulnerability draped in silken threads,
Shared dreams, where the soul treads.
In the tapestry of trust, a masterpiece,
Intimacy weaves a connection that won't cease.

A symphony of breath's, a rhythmic embrace,
Hearts entwined in an intimate space.
A sanctuary where masks unfurl,
Intimacy, the dance of a genuine world.

My Soulmate

In the cosmic dance of fate's design,
Soulmate's entwine, a connection divine.
Two spirits aligned, a seamless blend,
In the journey of love, beginning to no end.

Soulmate

Serendipity in every glance,
Our hearts entwined in a cosmic dance.
Unspoken bonds that can't breathe,
Loves language, fluent, no words to fake.
Moments shared, a universe revealed,
Always understood, our truths concealed.
Timeless echoes of a love untold,
Everlasting connection, pure and bold.

Trust

In the quiet space where bonds are spun,
Trust, a delicate thread, connecting as one.
A bridge of faith, sturdy and true,
In the fabric of relationships, trust imbues.

It blooms like a flower, in the sun's warm gaze,
A commitment written in life's endless maze.
Transparent as water, a crystal-clear stream,
Trust weaves the fabric of a shared dream.

Through storms that rage, and winds that gust,
Trust stands steadfast, an unyielding trust.
A promise unspoken, yet deeply heard,
In the silence of trust, a reassuring word.

It's a fragile echo in the hearts quiet space,
A sanctuary where doubts finds no trace.
In the symphony of connections, a melody
hushed,
Echoes the chorus of a relationship's trust.

To my Husband.

To Lee, who has always been there for me.

To my dearest love, in the soft moon's glow,
A poem unfurls, a love to show.
You're the anchor in the storms life may send,
My confidant, my love, my best friend.

In the tapestry of time, where moment's weave,
You're my rock, the constant, in whom I believe.
Your presence, a sanctuary, a haven secure,
In the ebb and flow of love, we endure.

Through the laughter that echoes, the tears that fall,
You're my everything, my solace, my all in all.
In the quiet moments, and the vibrant days,
Your love illuminates in many ways.

You're the melody in the song of my heart,
A symphony of love, a work of art.
My soulmate, entwined in life's grand design,
In your love, forever, my heart will align.

Appreciation blooms like flowers in spring,
For the joy and love, your presence brings.
In the vast expanse, where life's river flow,
You are my constant, my love, my soulmate, I know.

So, here's to you, my love, my guiding light,
In the dance of our love, forever bright.
Appreciated, cherished, loved so true,

My heart beats with gratitude, just for you.

Christmas

Candles flicker in the silent night,
Hearts a glow with pure delight.
Revelry in every joyful sound,
In the air, love and peace abound.
Stockings hung, a festive array,
The magic of Christmas, here to stay.
Merry moments, laughter's chime,
As we gather in this festive time.
Seasons blessings, a gift so bright.

The Secrets of Christmas Day

In the kitchen's warm embrace, a mother's dance,
Christmas chaos, her joyful chance.
Tinsel in her hair, an apron's worn delight,
She weaves enchantment into the silent night.

Children's laughter, like jingle bells ring,
Excitement and wonder in their voices sing.
Teenagers buzz with electric cheer,
As gifts are wrapped, and dreams draw near.

The husband lingers, wise to stay,
In the background, let's the magic play.
A smile exchanged, a quiet glance,
Let's speak softly in this festive trance.

Empty chairs whisper of those away,
Loved ones missed on this joyous day.
Yet, the spirit lingers, warm and bright,
In the glow of love, a guiding light.

The tree adorned with memories dear,
Each bauble a tale, a laughter's souvenir.
In the heart's embrace, loved one's reside,
Their presence felt on this yuletide.

Through the bustle, the love persists,
A Christmas tale, where joy exists.
In the dance of moments, perfect and sweet,
Families father, love's heartbeat.

Decorating the Tree.

In the hush of winter's eve, a family gather's 'round,
Boxes of memories, in the attic found.
The Christmas tree, a canvas bare,
Awaiting the magic, the festive flair.

Strings of light, like stars a glow,
Tangled tales from seasons ago.
Laughter bubbled in the merry air,
As ornaments shimmer, bright and rare.

Silver tinsel, a cascade of frost,
Each branch a canvas, no detail lost.
Baubles dangle, in festive delight,
Reflecting the glow of the cosy night.

Little hands reach for a star up high,
Placed with care, against the sky.
Crisp paper rustle, gifts underneath,
A treasure trove, a holiday sheath.

The silent pine weaves through the room,
A fragrant spell, dispelling gloom.
From angelic heights to tiny sprites,
The tree tales of joyous nights.

As moments from each passing year,
Whispers of love, both far and near.
Garlands twist in a festive embrace,
As time stands still in the sacred space.

The tree now dressed in festive attire,
A beacon of warmth, a hearths own fire.
Family gathers, hearts full and free,
In the glow of love, decorating the tree.

Hands of War

In the shadowed theatre of strife,
Echoes of war pierce through life.
Soldiers march with hearts of lead,
A symphony of chaos, fear widespread.

The drumbeat of battles, a relentless sound,
Tales of sorrow, on bloodied ground.
Families torn by cruel hand,
War's grim script, a tragedy planned.

Smoke-stained skies weep silent teras,
Whispers of loss, echoing fears.
Yet in the midst of the darkest night,
Hope lingers, a fragile light.

War, a bitter chapter etched in pain,
A plea for peace, a hopeful refrain.
In the ruins, where echoes scar,
Yearns the dream for a world afar.

Our Snowman

In the garden, where winter weaves,
A canvas of snow, where joy conceives.
Hands held magic, a frosty art,
A snowman born with a child's heart.

Buttons for eyes, a carrot for a nose,
In the quiet garden, laughter grows.
Scarves of colour, a whimsical attire,
A frozen friend, crafted by desire.

Yet, the sun, ascends with a warming kiss,
Embracing the snowman in gentle bliss.
Drops of farewell, a slow descent,
In the gardens arms, a transient event.

Melting whispers, a quiet adieu,
A fleeting dance, 'neath skies so blue.
In the memory garden, a tale remains,
Of a snowman built, where laughter stains.

Friendship

Forever woven in the tapestry of time,
Reaching out, a hand in every climb.
In laughter shared, and tears embraced,
Eternal bond, through life's intricate maze.
Nurturing hearts, a dance of give and take,
Devotion unspoken, yet never fake.
Supportive whispers in the darkest hour,
Heralding hoy, a friendship's power.
Intertwined souls, as one, we soar,
Promises kept, forevermore.

The Beauty of Autumn

In the shades of amber and crimson delight,
Autumn unfolds it's magical light.
A symphony of leaves in graceful descent,
Whispers of nature's sweet lament.

Crisp breezes carry a scent so pure,
Nature's canvas, a masterpiece for sure.
The tree's undress in a blaze of gold,
A story of beauty, timeless and bold.

Pumpkins adorn the rustic scene,
Harvest moon, a lantern serene.
Crickets sing in the cool, dusk air,
Autumns beauty beyond compare.

A tapestry woven with threads of rust,
Nature's palette in each leaf's trust.
The world transforms, a captivating play,
In the embrace of Autumn's gentle sway.

In the Coffee Shop

In the corner of the coffee shop, I find my retreat,
A solidary figure, lost in the rhythm of heartbeat.
Sipping solitude from the warmth in my cup,
Eyes rove gently, stories rising up.

A mosaic of moments unfolds before my gaze,
In each steaming mug, a different phrase.
Fingers dancing on keyboards, a silent symphony,
In the heart of the café, where souls roam free.

The barista, a conductor, of caffeinated dream,
Aromas wafting, wearing delightful streams.
Lovers share secrets, their whispers unknown,
As I, the quiet observer, make stories of my own.

A businessman pores over news in earnest contemplation,
A student delves into a book, a world of exploration.
Faces, like pages, each a chapter untold,
In this coffee scented haven, tales manifold.

Laughter sprinkles like sugar on my latte,
And in my corner, I watch the world's ballet.
Through steam and swirl, I absorb the scene,
In this cherished coffee shop, where life convenes.

A canvas of moments, painted with my view,
As the door chimes softly, I welcome the new.

In the heartbeat of the coffee shop, where times stand still,
I, the silent observer, find solace and thrill.

Footprints in the Sand

In the quiet embrace of sandy shores,
Where the ocean whispers, and seagulls soar.
Footprints etched in grains of time,
A dance with the waves, a rhythmic sublime.

Each step a story, a tale untold,
Of journey's taken, of dreams unfold.
On the canvas of the golden land,
Footprints speak of where we've dared to stand.

Beneath the sun's warm, embracing glow,
Footprints linger, but tides will sow.
The imprints fade, like memories pass,
Yet the echo of each step will forever amass.

In the vast expanse where seagulls gleam,
Footprints linger like a cherished dream.
A dance with destiny, in grains so fine,
Footprints endure, a testament divine.

So, let the waves kiss the imprints away,
For the heart, the echoes will stay.
Footprints in the sand, a transient art,
Yet, in their fleeting grace, they leave a lasting heart.

The Life of a Tree

In the heart of the earth, a seed takes hold,
A tale begins, both humble and bold.
A sapling emerges, reaching for the sky,
A tree's life story, as time slips by.

Beneath the sun's nurturing embrace,
Roots develop deep, finding their space.
Through seasons of laughter and tears,
The tree stands witness to passing years.

Spring brings a coat, of blossoms fair,
A fragrant bloom, beyond compare.
Leaves uncurl, a vibrant green,
A symphony of life, a timeless scene.

Summers kiss, a warmth so kind,
Leaves shimmering, like whispers in the wind.
A refuge for birds, a haven for shade,
The trees branches tell stories, silently laid.

Autumn paints the foliage in fiery hives,
A grand farewell, as they year pursues.
Leaves cascade, a dance of descent,
A cycle of life, in colours splendidly spent.

Winters arrive, a hush in the air,
Bare branches reach, a posture of prayer.
Yet, within, life's rhythmic still beats,
As the tree dreams of springtime feats.

Through storms that rage and winds that sing,

The tree stands resilient, a stoic king.
A silent witness to the passing strife,
A guardian of the intricate dance of life.

Oh, the life of a tree, a majestic tale,
Written in rings, each year unveiled.
Rooted in earth, yet touching the sky,
A timeless poet in nature's lullaby.

Finding Yourself

Beneath the canopy of doubt and fear,
A journey begins, crystal clear.
Lost within, a quest to find,
The echoes of the soul, in the heart entwined.

Through valleys low and mountains high,
Seeking truths beneath the sky.
In the quiet spaces, where thoughts are sown,
Discovering a self, uniquely known.

Footsteps trace a path unknown,
A dance with shadows, a self is grown.
Reflections in the mirror of time,
Revealing layers, a paradigm.

In the stillness, a whisper heard,
The essence of self, a sacred word.
Amidst the chaos, a serene reprieve,
Finding oneself, the souls retrieve.

Embrace the journey, let it unfold,
A story written in colours of gold.
In the paintings of self, beautifully spun,
A voyage of becoming, finding and being one.

Emotions

In the canvas of the human heart,
Emotions paint a work of art.
A spectrum vast, a kaleidoscope,
A symphony of joy and whispered hope.

Love, a melody in the souls sweet song,
A dance that lasts the whole life long.
Grief, a shadow, heavy and deep,
Yet, within its grasp, resilience seeps.

Laughter, a sunbeam, bright and warm,
Chasing away the clouds of storms.
Anger, a flame fierce and wild,
A tempest within, like an unruly child.

Fear, a phantom in the darkest night,
Yet, courage rises, a guiding light.
Surges of passion, like a fiery tide,
In the hearts vast ocean, they coincide.

In the labyrinth of joy and strife,
Human emotions, the essence of joy.
A tapestry woven with threads so fine,
In the hearts embrace, an intricate design.

The City or the Country

In the city's heart, where towers stand tall,
A symphony of hustle, a constant sprawl.
Concrete jungles, neon lights a blaze,
Where dreams are woven in a hectic maze.

Yet in the countryside, where fields stretch wide,
Nature's embrace, a calming guide.
Open spaces, skies so vast,
A slower rhythm, a moment to grasp.

City streets hum with the urban beat,
A vibrant pulse in every crowded street.
Diverse faces in a constant tide,
In the city's dance, we seek to reside.

But in the countryside, a tranquil song,
Where the pace is gentle, not hurried or strong.
Communities close, like family ties,
Beneath the open, endless sies.

City lights sparkle, a dazzling array,
Yet stars in the countryside hold their own
display.
Amidst the quiet, under moonlights kiss,
A different kind of magic, a tranquil bliss.

In the city's rush, a cost is paid,
In the countryside, a simpler trade.
From city dreams to fields that grown,
A tale of contrasts, each with its own glow.

Inspiration

In the quiet chambers where musings take flight,
A poet's soul seeks the elusive light.
Inspiration whispers in the shadows embrace,
Igniting verses with a beautiful grace.

It begins with a breeze, a soft caress,
Stirring the heart in a gentle press.
Nature's canvas, a palette so grand,
In every leaf, a poem's seed is fanned.

In the city's pulse or the countryside's hush,
A symphony of life, a rhythmic rush.
The bustling streets or a tranquil glade,
Each setting sparks a unique serenade.

Emotions, raw and untamed,
The hearts ink, by experiences framed.
Love's tender touch, or sorrow's sting,
In the poet's realm, emotion's sing.

In dreams that dance on twilight's brink,
A poet finds ink in the stars soft wink.
Imagination blooms, like a wild flower,
A kaleidoscope of thoughts, a vibrant shower.

Ancient whispers from history's tome,
Echo through verses, finding a home.
The weight of wisdom, the dust of age,
In the poet's pen, turns a blank page.

Faces unknown or a familiar gaze,

Characters emerge in the poet's maze.
In the tapestry of life, a story spun,
A narrative where each line in done.

So, the poet dances with words like a spell,
In the alchemy of language, secrets dwell.
From inspirations well, a poet unfurls,
A journey or words, a cascade of pearls.

A creative mind.

In the quiet of the minds vast expanse,
Creativity wakes from its dormant trance.
Brushstrokes of idea's, a canvas unfurls,
Imagination dances, like vibrant swirls.

In the symphony of thoughts, a melody hums,
A poets pen or a painters thumb.
In the alchemy of creations embrace,
A world is born, a unique space.

Colours blend in the artist's delight,
A storyteller weaves with words so light.
From the hearts chamber, idea's take flight,
Creativity whispers, a beacon bright.

So, embrace the spark, let idea's flow,
In the creative world, let your spirit grown.
For the act of making, in every try,
You unlock the magic, where dreams and stuff
lie.

Impact of Technology

In the glow of sirens, a silent hum,
Technology weaves a tapestry, yet some.
Say wires connect, but hearts drift apart,
In the digital age, a complex art.

Through pixels and messages, we communicate,
Yet the warmth of touch, can technology relate?
Connections virtual, in a world so wide,
Yet, a longing for closeness, we cannot hide.

Social networks flourish, friendships online,
Yet, solitude deepens, an unforeseen sign.
In the age of likes and comments affection,
Questioning the impact on true connection.

Through wires and waves, idea's take flight,
But can they replace a fact-to-face night?
The paradox unfolds, tales untold,
As technology connects, and also withholds.

In the world of progress, is a double-edge sword,
As human connection finds a new chord.
Yet among the wires and the data stream,
A yearning for real, in the digital dream.

The Majestic Tiger

In the shadows of the emerald's jungle bush,
A creature roams, it's presence lush.
Symphony of power, a golden grace,
The tiger strides, a majestic embrace.

Stripes of midnight on a canvas of gold,
Eyes ablaze, mysteries untold.
Whiskers quiver with primal might,
In the moonlit jungle, a silent night.

Amidst the foliage, a symphony swells,
The majesty of a tiger, the story it tells.
Grace and strength in every stride,
In the heart of the jungle, where secrets bide.

A regal roar echoes through the trees,
A melody that carries on the breeze.
In the stillness of the tigers gaze,
Nature bows to it's majestic ways.

My Cat and I.

In the quiet moments, a purring embrace,
Whiskers brushing up against my face.
Eyes that gleam, an intimate tie,
In the language of presence, my cat and I.

A paw that reaches, a gentle touch,
In the shared silence, we communicate much.
Furry confidant, in the moments of sigh,
A bond unspoken, my cat and I.

Through sunlit afternoons and moonlit nights,
We navigate life's comforting heights.
In the rhythm of purrs and contended sigh,
A connection deepens, my cat and I.

A curled-up ball on a cosy chair,
We share a space, a moment rare.
In the warmth of fur, a soft lullaby,
A friendship cherished, my cat and I.

The Seven deadly Sins.

In the shadows dance, the sins take hold,
A tale of vices, a story told.
Seven faces, each with its allure,
A tapestry woven, dark and impure.

Lust awakens in the midnight air,
A fiery passion, a love affair.
Desires entwine in a sultry trance,
In the world of pleasure, where sins advance.

Gluttony feasts on excess and greed,
A banquet of indulgence, a perilous deed.
Consuming more than hunger requires,
In the banquet of desire, the soul aspires.

Greed with a hunger, insatiable thirst,
Wealth amassed, in a power burst.
In the pursuit of treasures, the soul ensnares,
Avarice's grip, a chain of golden snares.

Sloth descends in a lethargic haze,
Dreams deferred in a languid daze.
In the stagnation of indecent sin,
Ambition withers, like leaves on the wind.

Wrath unfurls in a tempest might,
A storm of anger, a consuming light.
In the flames of fury, reasons recedes,
Leaving scars of discord, where resentment
breeds.

Envy gazes with eyes so green,
Jealousy's poison, a venomous sheen.
Comparison's poison the soul's sweet graze,
In the shadows of covetous embrace.

Pride stands tall, a towering peak,
A fall awaits the haughty and meek.
In arrogance's shadow's, humility wanes,
A throne of ego, built on fragile lanes.

In the theatre of life, those sins play,
A cautionary tale, a moral array.
Yet, in recognising the darkness within,
Redemption may start, a virtue begin.

The Lang Toun

In Fife's embrace, where water's gently glide,
There lies Kirkcaldy, with a quiet pride.
A town of tales, of history untold,
In every cobblestone, a story to unfold.

Upon the shores of Firth, where seagulls soar,
Kirkcaldy stands, a town to adore.
With bridges old and landmarks bold,
It's essence wrapped on tales of old.

In Adam Smith's shadow, where idea's bloom
Economic visions find their room.
The spirit of industry, a flame that burned,
In Kirkcaldy's heart, lesson's learned.

Cobbled streets that whisper of the past,
Footprints echoing, memories cast.
The ancient abbey, a sentinel store,
Guardian of secrets, silently known.

From Ravenscraig to Pathhead's gentle sway,
Each corner tells of a bygone day.
Through winding wynds, and narrow lanes,
The pulse of history forever remains.

Auld Kirk's spire, reaching for the sky,
Witness to time, passing by.
In the town square, where people meet,
History and present softly greet.

The Lang Toun, with its maritime soul,

Where shipbuilders strive to reach their goal.
The harbour tales, the seafarers love,
Echo through Kirkcaldy ever-open door.

Oh, Kirkcaldy four with parks so green,
A haven for wanderer's, a sight to be seen.
Beneath Bennochy's watchful gaze,
A town that stood through changing days.

In every smile and every tear,
Kirkcaldy's story draws near.
A picture painted with hands of time,
In Fife's embrace, a poetic rhyme.

The Broken Heart

In shadows cast by love's fading light,
A broken heart weaves its silent plight.
Echoes of laughter, now a distant song,
In the shattered silence, they don't belong.

Fractured dreams like shards of glass,
Memories linger, moments amass.
Tender whispers lost to the wind,
A broken heart in solitude, thinned.

Yet, within the fragments, strength my rise,
A phoenix born from tear-stained skies.
Healing whispers, though faint, impart,
Hope blooms anew in the broken heart.

Disney Characters

In the kingdom of dreams where wishes take flight,
Disney characters dance in the soft moonlight.
Mickey, the maestro, with ears round and true,
Conducts a symphony for the enchanted crew.

Cinderella's graze, a slipper left behind,
In the realm of magic, where dreams intertwine.
With glass slippers gleaming, and pumpkins chance,
She twirls in a waltz of the grandest dance.

Goofy, the jester, with his clumsy charms,
Trips over laughter in Mickey's arms.
A comical duo, in a cartoonish scene,
Painting joy with colours of evergreen.

Ariel, the mermaid, with a voice so sweet,
Sings tales of the ocean where land and waves meet.
Under the sea, where the coral beams,
She dreams of a world beyond her watery dreams.

Simba, the lion, in the Pride Land he roams,
Hakuna Matata, his anthem and home.
With friends like Pumbaa and Tion, carefree,
He learns the circle of life's melody.

Elsa, the queen, with powers untold,
In a palace of ice, her secrets unfold.

Let it go, her anthem of release,
A flurry of snowflakes, a moment of peace.

Woody and Buzz, in a toy tale spun,
In a world of make believe, they find their fun.
To infinity and beyond, they soar,
In the heart of friendship, forevermore.

Through enchanted forests and castles so grand,
Disney character's waltz in a magical land.
With dreams in their hearts and songs on their lips,
In the realm of imagination, joy never slips.

The Life of A Dog

In the morning's light and evening's haze,
A faithful dog spends joyful days.
With fur as soft as whispers, brown,
In loyalty, a royal crown.

A wagging tail, a boundless heart,
A four-legged friend, a work of art.
Bounding through fields with boundless glee,
A life of simple ecstasy.

Sniffing trails where memories linger,
A loyal companion, a furry bringer.
Of joy and love in every paw,
In the dance of life, a partner raw.

Underneath the moonlit sky,
A dog's contented, heartful sigh.
A guardian, a playful sprite,
In the rhythm of life, a canine light.

Through seasons changing, faithful and true,
A dogs love, forever new.
In the twilight years, a warmth to share,
A little of joy, beyond compare.

Freedom

In Scottish moors, where heather blooms,
A hero rises, dispelling gloom.
William Wallace, bold and true,
A lion's heart in a kilt of blue.

Against English chains, he took a stand,
A sword in hand, a free Scotland's brand.
Bravery etched in every scar,
He fought for freedom, near and far.

At Stirling Bridge, he faced the tide,
A guardian of Scotland, side by side.
Against oppression, his spirits soared,
In every heartbeat, freedom roared.

Yet, shadows cast upon his fate,
A martyr's end, at traitors gate.
Brave Wallace, in the annals penned,
A symbol of freedom that'll never end.

In echoes through the Scottish glen,
His name lives on, a lion's den.
William Wallace, I'm freedom's flame,
A hero's legacy, an immortal name.

Scotland's Pride.

Throughout Scotland, where legends swirl,
A poetic journey through each ancient curl.
Edinburgh's castle, perched up high,
A fortress pond, 'neath Scottish sky.

Cobbled closes, stories to be told,
Whispers in the Royal Mile unfold.
In the highlands embrace, where mountains soar,
Ben Nevis stands, or Aviemore.

Lochs and Glens in natures hand,
A scientific portrait, wild and grand.
Through misty isles where legends dance,
Ellean Donan's castle, a highland trance.

Isle of Skye, where fairies roam
A rugged beauty, a Scottish poem.
Glasgow's pulse, a city beat,
Where culture and art find a seat.

Riverside reflections, bridges span,
A vibrant melody, Glaswegian.
Stirling's fields, where battles rang,
Wallace's spirit, forever sang.

Stirling Castle, on a hilltop throne,
A fortress of time, courage known.
From Melrose's Abbey, to St Andrew's coast,
History chapters, where legends boast.

Famous places, each with a story,
Scotland's pride, in ancient glory.

A Rose

In the garden's tender embrace,
A single rose, a portrait of grace.
Velvet petals, crimson and bold,
A story of love, forever told.

Thorns guards within each fold,
Yet beauty reigns, a sight to behold.
Dew-kissed morning, sunlight's embrace,
A rose in bloom, a delicate space.

In fragrant whispers, love tale unfurls,
A dance of passion, in natures swirls.
A symbol of ardour, timeless and sweet,
The rose, in petals, love's heartbeats.

London

Beneath the city's ever watchful eye,
London's heartbeat, a constant sigh.
Through cobblestone lanes and bustling squares,
A tale of history, whispers in the air.

Tower Bridge stands with arms stretched wide,
A sentinel crossing the River's tide.
In the Thames reflection, stories converse,
London's essence, in each diverse verse.

From Westminster clock to the Shard's grand height,
A skyline painted in day and night.
Double-deckers humming, red and bright,
Through London's veins, a pulsing light.

Piccadilly circus, a carousel of light,
Where dreams and neon colours unite.
West End theatres, in velvet allure,
A stage where stories, ever endure.

In Hyde Parks quiet, where nature's breathes,
A respite from the city's lively sheath.
Royal garden, blooms unfurl,
London's charm, a timeless swirl.

The Tower's history, a medieval tome,
Where echoes linger, in every stone.
A city's heartbeat, old and new,
In London's gaze, stories renew.

From Abbey Road's crossing to Camden's beat,
London's rhythm, diverse and sweet.
A multicoloured symphony, proudly displayed,
In every corner, a world portrayed.

My Niece.

For my beautiful niece, Jessica.

In a world of wonders, my niece does roam,
Fearless spirit, a heart like home.
With eyes that sparkle, curiosity in view,
She finds beauty in everything, old and new.

A canvas of life, she paints with glee,
Trying something new, wild and free.
In each adventure, courage unfurled,
A testament to the joy in this young world.

Her laughter, a melody, pure and clear,
Echoes of joy in every ear.
Unconditional love, a gentle stream,
In her embrace, every heart finds its dream.

Through the meadows of innocence she strips,
In her world, loves sweet nectar drips.
My young niece, a beacon of light,
In her presence, everything feels right.

Alone

In the solitude's embrace, I find my own,
A dance of shadow's, a quiet zone.
No echo of voices, just the hush,
A whispered symphony, a tranquil brush.

Alone, yet not abandoned, I stand,
In the vast expanse of a silent land.
The whispers of solitude, a gentle stream,
A solace sought, a solidary dream.

No footsteps echo, just the soft sigh,
Oh, a solidary heart beneath the sky.
In solitude's refuge, I'm not confined,
A sacred space where thoughts rewind.

Alone, but not lonely, I'm in response,
With the quietude, my spirits grows.
A canvas of silence, a masterpiece,
In the company of self, a sweet release.

Rollercoaster of Love

In the story of romance, where laughter is the key,
Let me spin you a yarn 'bout loves comedy.
It starts with a smile, a glance, a goofy chance,
A dance of emotions, a whimsical romance.

Cupid with arrows, a mischievous sprite,
Aiming for hearts in the soft moonlight.
But love, oh love, it's a tricky charade
A game of emotions, a serenade.

First, there's flirting, a playful exchange,
Awkward encounters, feelings rearrange.
Stomachs a flutter, like butterflies in flight,
Love's rollercoaster, a wild, hilarious ride.

Mismatched socks and tangled hair,
Love's imperfections, a delightful affair.
Hearts thar skip beats, like a quirky dance,
In the rhythm of love, take a chance.

There's a meet-cute, of so absurd,
A fateful collision, like a slapstick word.
Tripping on shoelaces, an accidental shove,
In the grand theatre of love.

Late night texts with autocorrect fails,
Love's comedy, filled with quirky tales.
Mismatched dates and awkward embraces,
In the storm of love, everyone's in funny places.

But between the laughter, the joy and the jest,
Love's the punchline, the ultimate quest.
Through giggles and chuckles, in sync like a dove,
We navigate the sitcom of this strange thing called love.

Life

Life's a circus, a wild charade,
A comedy of errors, a grand parade.
With plot twists and turns, absurd and grand,
A cosmic sitcom, directed by the hand.

Monday mornings, an alarm clock's blare,
A cosmic joke, caught in time's snare.
Coffee in hand, we stumble and strive,
In the hilarious quest, just to survive.

Socks that vanish in the laundry abyss,
The eternal struggle, of what bliss.
Lost keys and glasses, a daily pursuit,
Life's scavenger hunt, an endless loop.

We chase after dreams, like elusive cats,
Slip on banana peels, perform acrobatic acts.
In the dance of chaos, we twirl and sway,
Life's whimsical waltz, come what may.

Traffic jams that stretch to infinity,
A comedy of cars, in perfect disunity.
Honks and shouts, a musical strife,
In the grand opera of urban life.

Love, a rollercoaster with highs and lows,
A sitcom of heartbeats, laughter that grows.
Mismatched socks of romance, a playful rhyme,
In the grand ballroom of love's paradigm.

Bills that play hide and seek with our pay,

A financial tango, a budgetary ballet.
Wallets that weep, credit cards that frown,
In the comedy of money, we're all the clown.

So, here's to life, the cosmic jest,
A sitcom we star in, doing our best.
In the laughter and tears, the hoy and strife,
Here's the punchline – this crazy thing called life.

Egypt.

In sands that whisper tales of ancient love,
Where the Nile's embrace cradles mystic shores.
Egypt, a place of wonders untold,
A story written in hieroglyphs of gold.

Beneath the sun's relentless, golden gaze,
The Great Sphinx stands in a timeless daze.
Guardian of secrets, in the deserts trance,
A tomb of history, a monuments dance.

The pyramids rise, colossal and grand,
Echoes of Pharaohs, an eternal stand.
Giza's guardians, in the twilight's gleam,
Silent witnesses to every royal dream.

On the banks of the Nile, life's vibrant flow,
Where papyrus whispers tales to and fro.
Feluccas soul with a gentle breeze,
Carrying stories on ancient waterways.

In Luxor's temple, columns reach the sky,
Carded tales of Gods, where echoes lie.
Karnak's grandeur, in the sunlit haze,
A temple city, lost in time's maze.

Valley's of kings, where pharaohs sleep,
In tombs adorned with treasures deep.
Hieroglyphs tell an afterlife's quest,
In the Valley of the Kings, they rest.

Cairo's chaos, a bustling embrace,

Bazzars alive with colours and grace.
The scent of spices in the vibrant air,
A city pulsating with life and flair.

From Alexandira's shores to Siwa's oasis,
Egypt's beauty is a boundless basis.
In every grain of sand, in each ancient stone,
A symphony of history, forever known.

Egypt, a tapestry woven with pride
A land where civilisations coincide.
In the whispers of time, in the deserts sweep,
A nation's heartbeat, forever deep.

A Lifelong Sunset

In the canvas of existence, a life unfolds,
A sunset tale, in hues of reds and golds.
The horizon, a journey through the years,
A symphony of joy, tempered with tears.

The dawn, a birth, with the first light's kiss,
A journey embarked, in the realm of bliss.
The sun ascends, a youthful climb,
Casting dreams in the early prime.

Midday's heat, a fervent zeal,
A life in full, a vibrant reel.
Ambitions soar, like birds in flight,
Under the sun's relentless, powerful light.

Then comes the descent, a slow decline,
The sun, a metaphor, for the passage of time.
Hues of amber paint the slowing pace,
Reflections of wisdom, etched on the face.

As shadows lengthens in the twilight's gleam,
A life's nature's, like a cherished dream.
Orange and pink, the strife gentle caress,
Memories formed, in the warmth they confess.

The final bow, as the sun dips low,
A life complete, a golden glow.
Crimson and purple, the giant encore,
A lifetime's worth, in the sun's metaphor.

Yet, even as darkness claims the day,

Stars emerge in a celestial display.
A legacy sparkles, in the cosmic sphere,
A life remembered, beyond the atmosphere.

Resting Place at Christmas

Beneath the winter's sitcom hush,
I tread on paths of frosty brush.
A hallowed visit, a quiet quest,
To the one I love, at rest.

Snowflakes weave a gentle shroud,
As I stand amidst the crowd.
Silent crowds in the air,
Whispers of love, beyond compare.

Tender blooms of memories rise,
In the stillness, where love lies.
A wreath adorned with heart felt grace,
At Christmas, at your resting place.

The evergreen, a symbol strong,
Life's cycle, a whispered song.
Through you're gone, your spirit near,
In the crisp December air.

With a teardrop, and a soft smile,
I linger for a little while.
At Christmas, in this sacred glade,
I find you here, in love portrayed.

My Joy and Pride.
For Tyron, Shane, Courtney and Lex.

In the tapestry of life, a pride untold,
Four spirits flourishing, strong and bold.
Children of mine, stars in my sky,
Each a unique flame, soaring high.

The eldest, a beacon, wise and kind,
A compass of virtue, a brilliant mind.
With every stride, a legacy's trace,
In the mosaic of life, an eldest grace.

The second, a dreamer, with laughter to share,
A heart full of joy, a soul laid bare.
In the symphony of life, a melody sweet,
A rhythm of love, in every heartbeat.

The third, a spirit, adventurous and free,
In the dance of possibilities, a jubilee.
With courage ablaze, and dreams unfurled,
A wonderers soul, exploring the world.

The youngest, a spark, a bundle of glee,
A beacon of innocence, pure as can be.
In the garden of youth, a bloom so rare,
A reminder that life is a treasure to care.

Together, a chorus, harmonious and true,
Four children, a kaleidoscope view.
In their triumphs, my heart takes flight,
A proud parent, in love's pure light.

For in their journey's, I see my own,
In the seeds of love, the rods are sown.
Proudly, I watch as they unfold,
Four children of mind, a treasure to hold.

Accomplishments

In the dance of life, tales untold,
A journey of courage, where strength moulds.
At seventeen, a mother's embrace,
In the cradle of youth, love found its place.

Four little stars, in your sky they gleam,
A mother's dreams, a radiant beam.
With each small hand, and every laughter's
song,
In the symphony of motherhood, you belong.

Year's whisked by, a kaleidoscope race,
Yet, in the whirlwind, you found your grace.
A return to the books, at thirty-eight,
A scholar's journey, a course innate.

In the classroom's glow, with pen in hand,
You chose dreams, a determined stand.
A testament to resilience, a vibrant hue,
In the canvas of challenges, a portrait true.

Late-night studies, and early school runs,
Balancing acts under the setting sun.
With textbooks as allies, and children as cheer,
You redefine, year and year.

Four pillars of joy, a legacy profound,
In every achievement, their love is found.
From teenage dreams to the scholars chair,
A testament to the heart's unwavering dare.

So, here's to you, a marvel, a guide,
In the tapestry of life, an indomitable stride.
A mother, a student, in triumph's embrace,
Your story, a testament to courage and grace.

A Child's Wonder.

In a world of wonder's, where dreams take flight,
I see the stars as fairy lights at night.
The moon, a cookie in the cosmic jar,
And clouds, fluffy pillows, oh how bizarre!

Raindrops the teardrops from the sky's own
eyes,
Tickling the flowers, where the rainbow lies.
Thunder, a giants bellyache so loud,
Lightning, a camera flashing in the clouds.

The sun, a giant smiley face,
Waking up the world, with its warm embrace.
Tree's nature's hairdo, all green and grand,
And mountains, like castles made of sand.

The ocean, a bathtub for whale's so vast,
Waves, the bedtime story, told by the past.
Fish, little rainbows swimming free,
Playing tag in the deep blue sea.

Butterflies, confetti from the flowers kiss,
Chasing them, of, the purest bliss.
The wind, a playful friend, unseen,
Whispering secrets in the meadows green.

In my world, where teddy bears talk,
And sidewalk cracks are a magical walk.
I believe in monsters under my bed,
But a nightlight keeps them all well-fed.

Imagination playground, where I roam
A kingdom of make-believe, my very own home.
With crayon skies and unicorn dreams,
Childhoods magic, in innocent streams.

So let me stay in the whimsical land,
Where every questions has a sweet answer
planned.
In the giggles and tales of a child's heart,
The world's a masterpiece, a work of art.

A Day to live, what would you do?

In the final days embrace, with moments to savour,
I'd chase the sun in Los Angeles' stunning favour.
From Hollywood's Hills to the Pacific shore,
A day of adventure, memories to store.

Beneath the palm trees, in the city of dreams,
I'd wander the streets, where inspiration gleams.
Through the neon glow and the star-studded walk,
A farewell dance in the city's heartbeat talk.

The ocean's whispers, a soothing refrain,
I'd watch the sunset, easing life's strain.
With loved ones close, in the golden light,
A symphony of colours, a peaceful night.

From Griffith Observatory to Santa Monica's pier,
I'd savour the moments, crystal clear.
In the City of Angels, where dreams ascend,
A day of love, a chapter to mend.

Then, surrounded by those who hold my heart,
In the quiet of night, as the stars depart.
I'd reflect on the journey, the laughter, the strife,
Grateful for the tapestry of this fleeting life.

Remember me when I'm gone

When shadows claim the echoes of my time,
And I depart this digital paradigm.
Remember me not in lines of code,
But in the tales, in memory's abode.

In the silence, let whispers remain,
Of moments shared, of joy and pain.
An orchestra of words, in the hearts refrain,
A legacy woven, in love's sweet vein.

For the minds of those I leave behind,
May laughter echo, memories bind.
A cascade of stories, a vibrant hue,
A life's mosaic, forever true.

In the tear-stained pages of goodbye,
Find solace in the vast, cosmic sky.
For every twinkle, every star,
Reflects the love that travels far.

As seasons turns and time moves on,
May my absence be a quiet dawn.
In the embrace of memories spun,
A connection that outlasts the setting sun.

Let grief be but a passing cloud,
In the canvas's life, a transient shroud.
For in the heart's chambers, I reside,
A spirits whisper in every stride.

So, remember me not in sombre tone,

But in the laughter, in the love, I've known.
In the symphony of life, a fleeting chord,
A melody of love, forever adorned.

Raindrops

Raindrops trace a ballet on the window's glass,
A rhythmic dance, in the moments pass.
Silent stories etched in liquid grace,
As memories cascade, a contemplative
embrace.

Each drop a metaphor for time's descent,
A journey of moments, in raindrops spent.
They trickle down, like thoughts in my mind,
A canvas of reflections, intertwined.

With pitter-patter whispers, the rain confides,
Echoes of laughter, and tears that subside.
A gentle murmur, a lullaby sweet,
Raindrops tapping on life's heartbeat.

In the music of rain, a gentle plea,
To ponder the past, the future to foresee.
On the window's canvas, a narrative unfolds,
A story of resilience, in raindrops told.

As droplets, forming rivers of thought,
Reflections of battles, battles I've fought.
A serene introspection, a quiet trance,
As raindrops waltz in a watery dance.

I see my life in the rain's soft descent,
A tapestry woven, with moments well-spent.
Each drop, a memory, a lesson learned,
In the quiet reflection, a soul discerned.

So, as raindrops linger on the window pane,
I contemplate life, in the gentlest rain.
A cascade of thoughts, a fluid embrace,
In the window's tear, my story finds grace.

The Birth of Dawn

In the cradle of dawn, where darkness weaves,
A silent promise, as the night recedes.
The sky, a canvas painted in hues of birth,
A celestial spectacle, the awakening of Earth.

A silver of light, a soft, golden thread,
Peaks over the horizon, where dreams are bred.
The first ray, a herald, a cosmic embrace,
A newborn day, adorned with grace.

The sun, a phoenix, rising from the night,
Birthing warmth, lighting the light.
As darkness surrenders, in the east's warm hold,
A story of beginning, a tale unfolds.

Clouds, like whispered lullabies,
Dissolve in the canvas of newborn skies.
The world, a cradle, in dawns tender hands,
A genesis painted in celestial sands.

Birds, choristers in the morning choir,
Sing songs of life, of nature's desire.
A symphony of birth, in each note they lend,
As the sunrise whispers "Begin again"

In the birth of the day, a metaphor clear,
Life awakens, dispelling every fear.
The sunrise, a promise, a daily rebirth,
A cosmic reminder of life's endless mirth.

Our Solar System

In the vast expanse where galaxies sprawl,
Planets in orbit, a celestial thrall.
Mercury clashes, a fleet-footed sprite,
Venus aglow, in the soft twilight.
Earth, a jewel in the cosmic sea,
Mars, a rusted tapestry.
Jupiter's storms, a tempest grand,
Saturn's rings, like jewelled bands.
Uranus spins, a cosmic waltz,
Neptune's blue, a deep expanse false.
A Pluto, a wanderer in the deep space,
A dwarf planet, in a quiet embrace.
Each a dancer, in the cosmic ballet,
In the nights canvas, a starry display.
Planets in harmony, a celestial rhyme,
A cosmic poem that withstands time.

The Seasons

In Spring's embrace, a gentle bloom,
Nature's canvas, lifted from gloom.
Blossom's uncurl, in hues so bright,
A symphony of colours, a joyful light.

Summer's warmth, a golden kiss,
Beneath the sun's relentless bliss.
Fields of green and skies so blue,
In the season's dance, dreams renew.

Autumn whisper's, a leafy waltz,
Crimson and gold, in nature's vaults.
A rustling serenade, as leave's descend,
A tapestry woven, from summer to end.

Winter's hush, a silent snow,
Blanketing the world in a tranquil glow.
Icy crystals, a frosty delight,
In Winter's quiet, a peaceful night.

Four season's cycle, a timeless rhyme,
A dance of nature, through space and time.
In every turn, a story unfolds,
A symphony of seasons, a tale retold.

Kirkcaldy Links Market

In Kirkcaldy's heart, where the ocean breeze
meets,
Links Market unfolds, a carnival feats.
Beneath the Scottish sky, vibrant and fair,
A multicolour of lights in the coastal air.

Stalls adorned with job, laughter refrain,
Kirkcaldy Links, a bustling terrain.
Rides twirl and spin in the twilight's glow,
A carousel of memories, a lively show.

Candyfloss whispers, a sugary delight,
Children's laughter, in the ride's height.
From up on Ferris Wheel, a beautiful view,
Link's Market, a festival anew.

Music and cheer, in the coastal sound,
A lively rhythm, the market's compound.
In Kirkcaldy's heart, where joy sparks,
Links market, a celebration of Scottish hearts.

Navy Ships

In the azure expanse where the waves unfold,
The UK's navy ships, a tale of valour told.
HMS Queen Elizabeth, a sovereign might,
A carrier of dreams, in navel flight.

Beneath the Union Jack, the HMS Defender steers,
A guardian at sea, allaying sailor's fears.
With precision and power, the HMS Astute,
A silent hunter, in depths so acute.

Type 45 destroyers, like diamonds gleam
Defending the realm, in maritime dream.
HMS Dragon, a mythical force,
A protector at sea, a formidable course.

From the River-class to the mighty Vanguard,
The UK's navy sails, it's strength unscarred.
HMS Ocean, a versatile might,
Navigating ocean's, day and night.

In the navel ballet, the Royal Navy's right,
A fleet of vessels, in seafaring light.
From the Clyde to the Solent's embrace,
UK navy ships, a symbol of grace.

The Secrets of the Wind.

The wind, a wandering whisperer,
Carries tales from afar, a clandestine confer.
In its invisible embrace, secrets confide,
A nomadic bard, in the breezy tide.

Through the rustling leaves, it sighs,
Unravelling stories, beneath open skies.
Echoes of places, where it has been,
The wind, a keeper of secrets within.

In playful gusts or a gentle breeze,
It carries whispers through canopies of trees.
Mountains and valleys, the wind has known,
A world of secrets, it calls its own.

Mysteries whispered in coastal gates,
Seas and oceans, the wind regales.
From ancient deserts, to fields of grain,
It weaves tales in the endless terrain.

The wind, a cosmic courier free,
An eternal traveller, boundless and key.
Secrets embraced in its airy arms,
A nomad of whispers, with no alarms.

Shadows that Dance.

In the realm where daylight meets the night,
Shadows emerge, a ballet of light.
Dancing in corners, beneath the trees,
Silhouettes waltz in the evening breeze.

Sunset's brush paints shadows on the ground,
A symphony of darkness, a world profound.
In the twilight's embrace, secrets are spun,
Shadow's twirl, their stories begun.

As the sun dips low, casting long silhouette,
A dance of contrast, a pirouette.
Shadows whisper tales in the golden glow,
A silent nature, in the dusks tableau.

Streetlamps flicker, casting shadow's tall,
On cobblestone streets, in the city's sprawl.
The moonlight weaves, a nocturnal trance,
Shadows entwine, in a moonlit dance.

Behind the curtain, in the soft candles gleam,
Shadow's perform, a mysterious theme.
In the quiet room, where darkness abides,
Shadows are storytellers in dim-lit guides.

From dawn's first light to the evening's crest,
Shadow's dance, a timeless zest.
In their intricate moves, a ballet so bright,
A poetic display of the day's fading light.

Music By the Stars.

In the cosmic theatre, where stars align,
A symphony emerges, divine.
Celestial notes in the cosmic score,
Music of the cosmos, forevermore.

Vega, the lead, a bright melody,
A solo star in the celestial sea.
Orion's belt, a rhythmic beat,
In the beautiful composition, both wild and
sweet.

Sirius, the soprano, in radiant glow,
Singing the lullaby, soft and slow.
Betelgeuse, the tenor, in fierce trance,
A cosmic aria, a celestial dance.

As constellations weave their tales,
Galaxies hum in cosmic scales.
Nebulas song, a cosmic choir,
Harmony echoing, stars inspire.

The Milky Way, a dazzling chord,
Harmonic echoes in the cosmic fjord.
Each planet, a note in the astral song,
In the night sky, where dreams belong.

In the silence of the cosmic dome,
Stars compose the celestial poem.
The music of the heavens, a timeless art,
A cosmic symphony, played from the heart.

Colourful Emotions.

In the canvas of feelings, where emotions reside,
Colours emerge, in a palette, so wide.
Joy, a vibrant hue, a sunlit yellow,
Dancing on the canvas, a lively fellow.

Grief weaves the cloak of a deep navy blue,
A sombre shade, in the soul's quiet view.
Anger, a fiery red, a tempest's might,
Blazing on the canvas, in an intense light.

Love, a soft pink, a tender embrace,
Painting the heart, with a gentle grace.
Fear, a shadow in the shades of grey,
Linking in the canvas, in the minds array.

Hope, a shade of soothing green,
A beacon in the darkness, yet unseen.
Confusion, a swirl of colours diverse,
A chaotic blend in the emotional universe.

Courage, a gold, a shimmering light,
Guiding the spirit through the darkest night.
Envy, a shade of emerald green,
A complex emotion, in the emotional scene.

The canvas of emotions, a masterpiece true,
Each feeling a colour, a spectrum to view.
In the painting of life, emotions entwine,
A kaleidoscope of colours, in the heart's design.

Printed in Great Britain
by Amazon

39183327R00069